THE APPASSIONATA DOCTRINES
by David Citino

Cleveland State University Poetry Center

ACKNOWLEDGMENTS

The author wishes to thank the editors of the following periodicals, in which some of these poems first appeared.

AKROS: "Letter to Sister Mary Appassionata, America's Adviser to the Lovelorn"

BELOIT POETRY JOURNAL: "Sister Mary Appassionata's Lecture to the Eighth Grade Boys and Girls on the Things of this World, the Things of the Other"; "Sister Mary Appassionata Addresses the Psychic Research Guild of Marion, Ohio"

THE BENNINGTON REVIEW: "A Lesson in Anatomy" from "Sister Mary Appassionata Lectures the Pre-Med Class"

CHICAGO REVIEW: "Sister Mary Appassionata Lectures the Creative Writing Class: *The Evangelist*"

THE CHOWDER REVIEW: "Sister Mary Appassionata Lectures the Eighth Grade Boys and Girls: *A Concise History of Witchcraft*"

CINCINNATI POETRY REVIEW: "Sister Mary Appassionata Lectures the Architecture Class: *Doctrines of the Wall*"; Sister Mary Appassionata Lectures the Biology Class: *Historia Naturalis*"

CRAB CREEK REVIEW: "Sister Mary Appassionata Lectures the Health Class: *To Keep the Blood from Running Cold*"

CROTON REVIEW: "Sister Mary Appassionata Lectures the Journalism and Metaphysics Classes: *Who What Where When Why?*

DENVER QUARTERLY: "Sister Mary Appassionata Lectures the History Class: *Doctrines of Memory*"

DESCANT: "Sister Mary Appassionata Lectures the Bible Study Class: *Noah*"; "Sister Mary Appassionata to the Women's Studies Class: *An Angel Thrusts a Spear into the Heart of Saint Teresa of Avila*"

THE HOLLINS CRITIC: "Sister Mary Appassionata Lectures the History Class: *Life of the Saint*"

THE LITERARY REVIEW: "Sister Mary Appassionata Lectures the Biology Class: *Natural Selection and the Evolution of Fear*"

MISSISSIPPI VALLEY REVIEW: "Sister Mary Appassionata Lectures the Bible as Lit Class: *Meditations on the Life of Noah*"

NORTH DAKOTA QUARTERLY: "Sister Mary Appassionata Quizzes the Physics Class"; "Sister Mary Appassionata Responds to Questions from the Floor"

THE PLAINS POETRY JOURNAL: "Doctrines of the Breath" from "Sister Mary Appassionata Lectures the Pre-Med Class"

POETRY CANADA REVIEW: "Sister Mary Appassionata Lectures the Quantitative Analysis Class: *Proof of the Existence of the Soul*"

SAN JOSÉ STUDIES: "The Four Fluids" from "Sister Mary Appassionata Lectures the Pre-Med Class"; "Sister Mary Appassionata on the History of Heat"

SOUTH CAROLINA REVIEW: "Sister Mary Appassionata to the Home Ec Class"

SOUTH DAKOTA REVIEW: "Sister Mary Appassionata Lectures the Ethics Class"; "Sister Mary Appassionata to the Human Awareness Class: *One Fate Worse*"

SOUTHERN HUMANITIES REVIEW: "Sister Mary Appassionata Lectures the Eighth Grade Boys and Girls: *The Second Day*"; "Sister Mary Appassionata Lectures the Eighth Grade Boys and Girls on the Nature of Eloquence"

SOUTHERN POETRY REVIEW: "Sister Mary Appassionata Lectures the Creative Writing Class: *Life of the Poet; Or, the Storm*"

THE SUN: "Sister Mary Appassionata Lectures the Creative Writing Class: *Naming Everything Again*"; "Sister Mary Appassionata Lectures the Bible Study Class: *Homage to Onan*"; "Sister Mary Appassionata Lectures the Clinical Psychology Class on the Life and Death of Blessed Eustochium of Padua"; "Sister Mary Appassionata to the Bible in Translation Class: *Rites of Purification*"

TELESCOPE: "Sister Mary Appassionata on the Nature of Sound"

TENDRIL: "Sister Mary Appassionata Lectures the Eighth Grade Boys and Girls: *The Family Jewels*"; "From Exile, Sister Mary Appassionata Writes to the Creative Writing Class"; "Sister Mary Appassionata Explains to the Classics Class Why So Many of the Great Lovers, Heroes and Saints Were Shepherds"; "Sister Mary Appassionata Lectures the Social Behavior Class: *Friends, Those Who Love*"; "Sister Mary Appassionata Lectures the Natural History Class: *Love and Curse, the Wind, the Words*"; "Sister Mary Appassionata Speaks During the Retreat of the Eighth Grade Boys and Girls"; "Sister Mary Appassionata Lectures the Studio Art Class: *Doctrines of Nakedness*"

THE TEXAS REVIEW: "Sister Mary Appassionata Lectures the Folklore Class: *Doctrines of the Strawberry*"

WIND/LITERARY JOURNAL: "Sister Mary Appassionata Lectures the Home Ec Class: *The Feast*"; "Sister Mary Appassionata Addresses the V.F.W."; "Sister Mary Appassionata Addresses the Eighth Grade Boys and Girls During a Field Trip to the Museums of Natural History and Art"; "Sister Mary Appassionata Lectures the Eighth Grade Boys and Girls: *Flesh Willing, Spirit Weak*"

THE YALE REVIEW: "Sister Mary Appassionata Lectures the Eighth Grade Boys and Girls on the Life and Death of St. Teresa"

The first half of this volume, "The Appassionata Poems," was originally published as a separate book by the Cleveland State University Poetry Center in 1983.

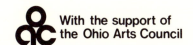

With the support of the Ohio Arts Council

for Mildred and John

CONTENTS

The Appassionata Poems

The Appassionata Doctrines

The Appassionata Poems

SISTER MARY APPASSIONATA LECTURES
THE EIGHTH GRADE BOYS AND GIRLS:
EVERY DAY ANOTHER SNAKE

And God gave Adam hands, fingers
smooth enough to soothe, deft enough
to create, arms long enough to reach,
but Adam sinned by trying to please
himself alone, so God made Eve, and
to her too gave hands, fingers, arms,
but Eve sinned by wanting to please
herself before all else, so God was forced
to make the snake, but by this time
He'd learned a lesson, and made it
limbless, and its slither and hiss
made Adam work, and Eve, until
their hands grew rough as pumice,
fingers gnarled from scrabbling for roots
in rocky soil, sewing greasy skins
callous-tough with blunt bone needles,
arms bent from a winter's weight
of firewood, a spring field's
depth of stone and clay.

Still today women and men come
into the world with the means to soothe,
create and reach, but a burning lust
to please nobody else. Every day
God's forced to make another snake.

SISTER MARY APPASSIONATA LECTURES
THE EIGHTH GRADE BOYS AND GIRLS:
THE SECOND DAY

When He said on that first dark day
"Give me light," there flew in
from nothingness legions of creatures
plumaged in sunshine, each pair of wings
a song. He gave them names like "Basso"
and "Contralto," "Wind-in-Pines" and "Lark."
He spent the rest of the day listening.

But by the piercing dawn of the second day
the song fell apart, harmony wavering
and cracking, the heavens sounding like
a turntable with too many records piled on;
and He didn't care for the way some angels
sang to others, wings fluttering together,
on every cloud an act of brazen love.

So when He divided the waters under
the firmament from the waters above
the angels whose feathers grew dim with sweat,
wet with wanting and coarse enough to touch
could no longer fly, and fell terribly
from the sky, screams fading as they dropped
through air and earth and into fire.

Thus were demons created, numbering,
the Talmud tells us, exactly 7,495,926
though some believe each infant brings along
when he falls to earth another thousand.
This is how things got the way they are.
This second day alone of all the seven
of the week wasn't called "good."

SISTER MARY APPASSIONATA LECTURES
THE EIGHTH GRADE BOYS AND GIRLS:
THE FAMILY JEWELS

In the beginning He put man's parts
of love where today you find the nose,
and woman's where her mouth is now.
But she grew too lean and hungry;
he couldn't stop sneezing. Loving,
they couldn't catch their breath.
Neither could get a word in edgewise.

So He put them where today you find
the hands, but it became too hard
to separate the gestures of friends
and lovers. An embrace came to mean
too little, a handshake much to much.
The tribes couldn't discern work from play,
war from peace, itch from scratch. So

He put the instruments of love where
they belong, mouth for ardor, zeal
and pleas, nose for scents, hands
to make or break, give and take, things
of passion closer to the heart than
brain, veiled as all great beauty
must be. Hidden from the greedy

and profane, the family jewels.

SISTER MARY APPASSIONATA LECTURES
THE BIBLE STUDY CLASS: *NOAH*

Months and months adrift
and more marooned on a mountain
in a leaking, three-storied boat of gopher wood
filled with his family,
all clean animals by sevens, unclean
by twos, stench of beasts, mildew and pitch
a powerful perfume wafting to heaven,
incense of all flesh.

The first forty days they hated Him, hearing
beyond bellow and babble below
and rain on the roof loud as static
on a stormy night
the faint cries of those they floated by,
whose only sin was to be born
outside the covenant.
One by one the unbelievers lost their grip
or grew too faint to stroke and kick
and slipped back into the sea
all life once had crawled from,
lungs and fingers a useless evolution.

Then it stopped. Hate became fearing,
then vigilance and resolution. It was
the most precious cargo ever to float.
They had to love, and love again.
Hating could only mean another storm.
They were the world compressed to three hundred cubits
by fifty by thirty,
one jagged rock, tree or temple-top
from joining the bloated things
floating toward them and away
white as bone, as salt.

House of all seed, memory and gene,
every last word, there was nothing for them but
to practice being fruitful.

Even the beasts recognized the obligation,
screaming elephants plaiting trunk and tail
into lovers' knots, camels undulating
humps, rocking the boat
with their lumbering enthusiasm,
sparrow, dragonfly and crow,
nighthawk and finch in twos reckless
in air, rabbit, pig, goat and dog
glassy-eyed, love an essence, pulse, hunger,
every male rigid as death
minute by minute, females damp as April dew,
flopping about like trout out of water,
coming together for all they were worth,
dancing over the killing waves.

In those days, not to exceed
their parents' voyaging,
not to last just long enough, was to perish.
Learning to keep afloat
just above danger, like the dove in search of olives,
they taught us generation,
and that endurance always comes in pairs.

SISTER MARY APPASSIONATA LECTURES THE HUMAN BEHAVIOR CLASS:
ONE MOUTH, LOVE AND ACHE

Because God put in one mouth
both tongue and teeth, each of us
must give and take both love and ache,
wear the masks of song and snarl,
learn how often words are made to break.

SISTER MARY APPASSIONATA LECTURES
THE EIGHTH GRADE BOYS AND GIRLS
ON THE NATURE OF THE CANDLE

*There are many instances during the Middle Ages of persons
having a candle made, as a special devotion, of the same
height or the same weight as themselves.*
                              —*Curiosities of Popular Customs*

It stands to reason. Wax crafted by bees,
tallow of vegetable or beast rendered just hard enough
to stand, to support the flame that dances
dangerously before the slightest breath, wick
running the body's length, spinal cord
that makes all parts a whole, intelligence
warming whatever comes near, touch of love,
to dispel the sentence of night after night,
only need to be, but eating a hole
in the center, faith consuming flesh from the inside,
running toward the heart, a fuse,
utter dark biding its time under the tongue,
inside each tooth and bone, life drowning
in the rising tide of life, deadly depth
of every day, price we're made to pay
for our season of light, last breath
a hiss or sigh as sun floods windows
to bear the soul away, what's left of us lying
gutted, guttered, cold, scents
of our brief wisdom lingering in the room.

SISTER MARY APPASSIONATA LECTURES
THE SCIENCE CLASS:
FOSSILS, PHYSICS, APPLE, HEART

Fossil bones, splintered bits of pelvis,
jawbone, tooth and skull aren't
of early apes and men
but of fallen angels made by greed too gross
to fly, who shattered when they hit the ground.

We know from physics every clock
winds down, each woman and man lies down
one more time than necessary for sleep or love.
Every movement culminates in stone,
each light and life in the ocean of night.

Drowned bodies, drunkards, heroes, saviors
surface always on the third day.

Virgin wool cures the deepest ache or burn.

Girls with big breasts and too much heart won't
fit into heaven. The boy who can unclasp
a girl's brassiere with one hand
knows too much for his own good
and all his life will have his hands full,
his mouth open at the wrong time.

The key to happiness? Knowing every second
of every day what to do with the hands,
when to loose or hold the tongue.

The holiest creatures are those that fly. God
Himself's part falcon, cuckoo, pelican, dove.

The girl who indulges herself
by climbing spiked fences, riding a horse
with too much passion, stooping too often
to pick mushroom or orchid

or dreaming of lovers who feel as she does
will from the wedding night on
be too easy on her husband.

Man's the only animal dumb enough to try
to cry back the dead, take
another's life only out of spite,
give his life for love.

Those whose eyebrows meet can never be trusted.

Women named Agnes always go mad.

No hunger justifies eating an apple
without first bringing it to life by breathing
on it, filling it with beauty
by rubbing it across the heart.

SISTER MARY APPASSIONATA LECTURES THE SEX EDUCATION CLASS: *DOCTRINES OF THE KISS*

Behold the birds of the air, how
they bill and coo, the nuzzling
of beasts in each field, elephants
even, braiding lumbering trunks.
Observe cats licking kittens, dogs
how they sniff, baboons groom.

Homer, wise as he was, was blind
when it came time to kiss. Celts
could find no word for it.
Egyptians taught us how to inhale
at one another to unite two souls.
Eskimos, Maoris and Malays press

noses. One Yakut rubs another's
cheek with cold, cold lips, then
waits for inspiration. The French
sin with the tip of the tongue,
grow so hot together they lose
all sense of up or down. Babies

and lovers suckle and bite,
mothers and lovers peck, heal our
every wound. It's the way we set
our seal, make peace, betray
another's savior or mate, bring
ourselves luck, take leave of

our senses, comrades. When we
kiss, every sleeping beauty grows
aroused for dawn, each frog becomes
charming prince. The kiss
makes one of two, involves all ten
senses: savor and feel, love's

scents, whisper and tongue, look;
yet nothing we do, no gesture
makes us more ethereal, gets us
farther from the solitary hell of
bone. When we give our lips away
we're never more ourselves.

SISTER MARY APPASSIONATA LECTURES THE SEX EDUCATION CLASS: *HISTORIA SEXUALIS*

In every drop of semen are seven-times-seventy
angels, golden, man-warm and God-faced, who
use their wings to swim. Each egg
inside a woman bears a portrait of the Virgin.

To see where one so lovely came from, Nero
slit open his mother's belly,
made a shrine of her pelvis.

St. Peter appeared to Agatha in prison
just before she was torn apart
to return to her on a silver plate
the breasts she'd lost the night before
to a Roman and his stubby sword.

Who knows the size of a man's nose
knows the length and circumference of the art
that grows below.

When Adam lost his rib he also lost
the hair that flourished on his palms.

If every act of passion together or alone
didn't cost a year of life
women and men would live forever.
If you move together, as you were made to do,
you must wait for one another. At the instant
of sharpest joy a year of life's exchanged.
If you accept this gift before the one
you're with gets his or hers, you've sinned
the greatest sin and must, the moment strength
returns, begin to move again.

SISTER MARY APPASSIONATA LECTURES THE EIGHTH GRADE BOYS AND GIRLS ON THE NATURE OF ELOQUENCE

German tribes hung the heads
of their most eloquent dead
in trees, where, open-mouthed,
they'd sing as long as bone
endured to the rhythms
of God's endless waltz, the wind.

Kleomenes of Sparta kept the head
of his most trusted friend Archonides
in a honey jar, to consult
in times of crisis, for when
things are most bitter
no counsel's sweeter than that
of one who's loved beyond the grave.

The Irish mixed a fistful of brains
from a lost comrade with the earth
he shadowed and made bitter
by his fall, molding a weapon that,
when tempered by the fire and lament
of a long night's vigil, would live
again when flung, finding the murderer
by listening for his voice,
looking into his face, smart enough
to take a shattering revenge,
eloquent enough to shape a song
his sons would sing forever
after he fell back to dust and clay.

SISTER MARY APPASSIONATA LECTURES THE CINEMATOGRAPHY CLASS: *LATE, LATE MOVIE*

During each black and white frame
of *It Came From Beneath the Sea*,
while lovers walk about in twos
or threes, climb stairs together,
lock and bolt their doors,
the ocean moans just behind or below,
hisses slowly up the beach where
they lie entwined, a brackish greed
seething weedy and shrill, a rage.

But the breathless truths of those
who've glimpsed the thing
about to slither and roar through
its rites ashore are thought
too passionate, mad. Waves
conquer the harbor in time. Scene
after scene, each actor becomes
an island. The sea screams to be
heard over rising violins, god

who's come back for his children.

SISTER MARY APPASSIONATA LECTURES THE CREATIVE WRITING CLASS: *NAMING EVERYTHING AGAIN*

. . .and whatsoever Adam called every living creature, that was the name thereof.

We're designated to travel
from a world where nothing needs
a name to this, where all things cry out
for one. *Cleveland, Ohio.*
Ascension of Our Lord Church.
Giovanni. John. Father.
Eastern Daylight Saving Time.
Undertaker.
Extreme Unction.
Heart.
Beat.
We're made to describe the way
from dark and silence to here,
through every letter, to learn that,
sure as night defines the day, to be
means naming everything again.

SISTER MARY APPASSIONATA LECTURES
THE HOME EC CLASS: *THE FEAST*

On time for every meal
whether I set them a place
or not, the family ghosts
assemble around the table.
My parents and theirs, dead

uncles, cousins and friends
light as steam, subtle as
anise, bay leaf or sage,
study me as I pierce and carve,
slice and chew, pause to savor.

Grease of flesh stains lips
and fingertips, coats teeth
and tongue as rust does iron
or dust the porcelain figurines
in the proper homes of

proper old ladies. Course
after course, meal after meal
and still they're unsatisfied.
Grandfather, speck of oregano
stuck between front teeth,

wipes sauce red as heart's blood
from his plate with a crust,
holds up a glass to ask for
more wine. "But you can't be
thirsty," I whisper. We're

destined to meet like this
three times each day, the family
become a rite, a thirst we'll
never slake, hunger ever
unappeased, our need, the feast.

LETTER TO SISTER MARY APPASSIONATA, AMERICA'S ADVISER TO THE LOVELORN

Q.
My husband's heart's gone
fat and blind, heavy
as a side of beef twisting
slowly in an icy locker,
ham hocks and pork snouts
in the market's cooler, lungs
porous as torn cheesecloth,
two handfuls of greasy suet,
tongue rough as the bull's.

Where love once reared
its proud red head a lamprey
wriggles, limp as old garden hose.
There was a time he could blast
off its silver maple limb
a new brown squirrel
at two hundred yards. Now
he can't see a thing below his
belly. What do you advise?

A.
Every dream disobeyed
becomes by light of dawn
a wound, five pounds more
of ache: lungspot, heartclot,
stone stuck up duct, clogged glands,
chilled glans, handfuls
of vandal cells rioting through
a body's bourgeois avenues.
Heed the dreams, love, you'll

make him over again.
Saved by the all-too-human need
to sleep and dream at the same time,
you'll learn what to wear, where
to have the hole dug, how to
lower him away under stone in a spray
of holy water and tears, cut mums,
poppies, lilies, baby's-breath.
In time all milk turns, meat goes bad.

Soon enough you'll be one again,
sweet and fresh, everlasting. Like death.

SISTER MARY APPASSIONATA LECTURES
THE HISTORY CLASS: *LIFE OF THE SAINT*

All his life it hurt like
ice on a bad tooth to live
in the body: lungs gravel-loud,
throat scalding at each inclination,
bones kindling-brittle when he

misstepped or, trying to cast off
too soon, was yanked back to earth.
The toughening, savage heart arrhythmic,
each silence between beats
a premonition, always too fast or slow

for him to keep in step yet
not once overtaking desire.
The magic wand between the legs,
stately pine or limp garter snake
at the worst of times, its will

his own. He saw at once what
depth and breadth meant to the deer,
the sparrow and calf, the trout,
mouth snapping shut on the hurt
of its last supper. His parents

grew to hardened hearts, bags
of precious wind, bushels of teeth,
hair, bone, guilt and rings. Flesh
a target of every barbed hunger,
one more than it could elude at last,

the weight, darkness he was made to bear.

SISTER MARY APPASSIONATA LECTURES
THE BIBLE STUDY CLASS: *HOMAGE TO ONAN*

Resurrection man, father
of the race and genocide,
puppeteer playing God,

you're empty gesture,
open hand a blessing, fist
a curse. As powerful

nearly as the one who
waits with finger on button
poised to end it all

with the biggest bang.
Impossible as the needle
through the camel's eye,

love born dying at your feet.
What's the sentence to fit
such crime? As part of

your passion, to endure
whenever alone desire's
shivering frictions until

you're worn out, to bear
the unbearable weight,
gravity of humanity, to

stumble down streets
thronged with lovers fit
for one another, those who

didn't fail, to move to death.

SISTER MARY APPASSIONATA LECTURES
THE RELIGION AND MYTHOLOGY CLASSES:
FROGS AND FORESKINS, HEART AND TONGUE

A frog from Egypt's plague, piece of reed
from baby Moses' yacht. Two lumps of lard—
what's left of Lawrence and Joan. A piece
of Shadrach's unsinged robe. Pine shavings
curlicued from Joseph's plane, sawdust
from his rasp, divine chips off
the old block. The Bambino's foreskin.
Feathers from Noah's dove, droppings from
the one that blessed the Apostles' tongues,
the raucous jay Francis shut up with his
simple singing. Feathers from
the engendering wings of Gabriel.
Wormy core of Adam's unswallowable apple.
Comb from the cock that crowed to reproach
Peter. Bones from Balaam's
eloquent ass. Feet of four and twenty crows
knocked out of the sky by Loreto's
high-flying house. Pickled in a canning jar:
Lucy's most discerning eyes, Agatha's nipples,
the herring bone Blaise made the boy cough up,
whole and unaltered hymens of Veronica
and Mary, Holofernes' ear, Cecilia's
vocal cords, heart and tongue of Isaac Jogues,
Abel's skull, irreparably shattered.
A quart of milk from Mary's right breast.

We can't be damned for not believing in these;
only for being so cocksure this world's
a place narrow as the space between our own
eyes and ears, death's-head cell of darkness and bone,
hell of thinking always only that we know.

SISTER MARY APPASSIONATA LECTURES
THE CLINICAL PSYCHOLOGY CLASS
ON THE LIFE AND DEATH OF
BLESSED EUSTOCHIUM OF PADUA

Most of the townsfolk who clumped
each night around the convent wall like
leukocytes around an infection
and demanded that she be shut up for good,
most thought her possessed
of too little morning, too much night.
Daughter of a nun who had no alms
to give a handsome beggar
and no qualms about giving herself instead,
she was always mother's little girl,
confusing give and take, in and out,
love and love. Her pious smiles adorned
the curses she recited each time some demon
slipped between her lips
to waltz and polka her around the floor.
She once was found alone in her cell
naked as Jesus in the manger, eyes
shut tight but smiling the smile
you don't get from dreaming.
The sisters, turning their faces to avoid
the devotion and despair wedded
in her eyes, tried to make her pure again
with the fire of the scourge. How such
holiness hurt her isn't recorded.
After death the embalmers read
with trembling fingers just below the breast
the scarred letters in a child's hand,
J E S U S. She's patroness of those
pulled apart by gravities of earth and sky,
all who're not themselves alone, emblem
of the darknesses that frame each day.

SISTER MARY APPASSIONATA LECTURES
THE CREATIVE WRITING CLASS:
THE EVANGELIST

John, Zebedee's son, best writer
of the twelve, you made Him, then
with a critical eye watched Him
shiver and mope through the final supper,
learned His voice and hate for the state
so well you made them your own,

until years later, head nodding
with the fleeting certainties of age,
you filled a book with sixes and sevens,
locust and scorpion swarming over
sinners who winked at revelation,
giggled at anything you had to say.

Preaching to Rome's Senate
from your cauldron of bubbling oil,
finding yourself unable to die
with so many manuscripts unpublished,
you taught us writing justifies
doubt and loving, showed us

words are always our salvation.

SISTER MARY APPASSIONATA LECTURES
THE THEOLOGY CLASS
ON THE LIFE AND DEATH OF ST. TERESA

She's become a journey.

Her left arm's at Lisbon,
fingers of the right hand at Seville, Avila, Paris,
Brussels, Rome.
Right foot in Rome, a slice of flesh.
One tooth in Venice.
Piacenza boasts of a napkin stained with her blood.
Milan keeps a piece of the heart, another tooth.
Lump of her flesh in Naples, scapular.
Her slippers at Avila,
most of the torso at Alva,
at Cagliari her veil.
The wooden cross she used to beat the demons
sent to try her, at Rome. Also Brussels.
Two very large slices of flesh in Krakow.

She lived to keep herself intact.
At the instant of death love tore her to pieces.

SISTER MARY APPASSIONATA LECTURES
THE CREATIVE WRITING CLASS:
LIFE OF THE POET; OR, THE STORM

She spent that night shivering
the storm away in the enormity
of her bed, hands clenched
between legs, carried away by dream.

He looked like Jesus, face contorted
by passion and thorn. He smelled
of gin. He carried something
like a tree, one end scraping

a furrow in the dusty street.
His sandals slapped the soles
of his feet as he walked. She
followed, two steps to every one

of his, but gained no ground.
A hot wind hit her like a horrible idea.
She swelled at bodice and hip. "My
little girl," he said, but her profile

gave her away. He put something
against her, took her breath away.
So suddenly she was all woman. What
hurt her so when she awoke was that

nothing had changed. Every night
since, she wakes at least once to
the roaring of heartbeats, blood, bed
quaking with thunder, fighting for air

in a room loud with winds of words,
the storm consuming her outside and in.

SISTER MARY APPASSIONATA PROVES TO THE ENTOMOLOGY CLASS THAT WOMAN AND MAN DESCENDED FROM THE CRICKET

Our mother and fathers,
sojourners in bogs, architects
of prairie clods, perennials
strewn over mountainsides,
forders of rolling creeks, herds,
loving under thatch and star,
each word together a bellows
heartening the flame, sang
to summer rain and generation,
feared only the sudden shrill bird
of fire or wind. Where they fell
cities were raised. We lost our ear
to concrete and brick, thick rivers
stagnant under iron spans, tug
and barge contending with siren,
horn, raucous hell of press, mill,
forge. Tonight just beyond
the bedroom wall our parents and the wind
will return to soothe earth's
August fever with a cool hand,
remind us of love's sympathetic magic,
leaping and creaking from clump
and bush, thick weedy field,
chanting the history of the world.

SISTER MARY APPASSIONATA LECTURES
THE THEOLOGY CLASS
ON THE RESOURCEFULNESS OF DEMONS

When it's time for study
they hang on my eyelids,
remind me of Chablis'
sweet French kiss, make the window
a shade too enthralling. They
take up residence under the tongue,
and when I most need to be
an inspiration I'm made
to stutter, hem and haw. One
sits between my legs, and when
I'm in the middle of abstinence
and beauty strides into the room
on muscled thighs, imposing
itself between decades of the rosary,
makes outrageous demands, upsetting
the fragile balance I've
struggled to erect. In the library
they turn pages dark
with the laughter of lark and jay,
tittering of children
in the garden that's summer, bark
and whine of distant dogs. Much as we do,
a demon's what we leave undone. Far
as we go, a demon lies an inch
beyond, taunting. I know
where they've been by the wrinkles and creases
of a hot night's sleep, by what's left
in the bathwater when I rise steaming and clean.

SISTER MARY APPASSIONATA RECOUNTS
A FOLKTALE

No, no, no, no she said, squirming
beneath the convertible top
of the '57 Chevy, hemmed in
by his more experienced words,
defter hands. Out in the night
the brooding, drooling one-handed
danger the radio said had just escaped
stalked them both, but he was breathing
too loud for her to hear. *I'm*
saving myself. Take your hands
away. Take me home now please.
He did, the ache of teenage love denied
nearly doubling him over the wheel
each time he had to clutch or brake.
They found her father robed on his lawn,
hands on hips like some angry god,
enraged over rainbow bruises
on his little girl's throat,
the wrinkled skirt and angora sweater,
stains of mortal passion on his pants
and, just above where she sat, stuck
in the car's rag top, time's
glittering awful weapon lovely and lethal
as a scythe, the hook.

SISTER MARY APPASSIONATA LECTURES THE FOLKLORE CLASS:
DOCTRINES OF THE STRAWBERRY

Mary, full of the mercy only
mothers know, hides the souls
of unchristened infants, guilty
as sure as they're born, in seeds
of strawberries, Jesus' favorite fruit,
and when He's picked and had His fill,
walking out into heaven's
misty meadows and groves weeping over
the gross appetites of the wicked,
thinness of the good, and after
nature's run its course, their beauty
passing through Him like too much
of any good thing, the seeds are left
to be covered with the dirt of paradise,
time's never ceasing tide, but soon
to rise again in blossoms of white flower
and plump red fruit, bitter and sweet
as blood, as life,
waiting for Him to come again.

SISTER MARY APPASSIONATA LECTURES THE EIGHTH GRADE BOYS AND GIRLS ON THE THINGS OF THIS WORLD, THE THINGS OF THE OTHER

1.
God's at the bottom of the Sea of Japan,
a giant catfish old as darkness, slumbering
in fecund ooze, compost of creation, slimy
as liver. He dreams the world. Each twitch

of His whiskers, fins and tail means
another city leveled, another ten thousand
in over their heads. Civilizations go
to sleep each night praying God won't stir

or flop, make waves; won't, raging, rise.

2.
In every sudden winter river, God's what
hardens, that beast and man might stiffly
walk or glide across, a miracle,
each exhalation an aura, halo of holiness.

God's what sizzles the frying egg from clear
to white, garlic's spinning hiss, blight
that hastens falling fruit, earth's kiss dark
as a bruise, awful hardness that seizes

every lover, corpse, His sticky seed our dew.

3.
The Pharoah's personal physician was called
Shepherd of the Royal Anus, which goes
to show that sometimes gods move in
the commonest ways, words made flesh. Jesus

spat at blind men just to make them see.

4.
Rue cures the horniest witch's curse,
shrivels the lecher's stiff and massive passion.
Weasels and priests feed on its leaves
before going out to charm the snake.

Exorcists steep a leaf in blessed water

to tempt young girls from toadstools, scald
the throat of one possessed, sealing
the demon's blaspheming lips. In times of dread,
piles of smoldering dead, place it in church,

the baby's bed, near every mirror, fire,

it clears the head. Girls, put it where
your latest lover was, to draw out the ache
of generation. Life's a loss. Spend each day
adding, subtracting, recounting the expulsion

from the garden. Brew a cup of tears. And rue.

5.
The eyes shoot rays that photograph the world, no matter
how bad the composition, the light. Pius IX, good
and well meaning as they come, had the evil eye. He once
looked a baby out of its mother's arms high above Rome's
cobblestones and watched it plummet to earth, a fat,
ripe melon. When he blessed, walls went out of plumb,
mortar was changed back to water and sand, laborers fell
screaming from heaven, scaffolding collapsing like
cards. Ships and virgins went down like tons
of bricks. Only a greater gift can guard against
the evil eye. Mussolini kept his hands in his pants pockets
when Alphonso of Spain came to see him. He knew a handful
of the family jewels can soothe the wound of sight,
overcome the most glittering malice. If in the last six months
you've shed no tear, God will fill your eyes with cataracts.

Still today we veil widows and brides, spend our hard-earned
coins on the eyes of the dead. My own father died
of a broken heart because his mother stared at a picture
of the Sacred Heart on the bedroom wall as her husband labored
above her to plant the seed, her cries of love a prayer.
Because of the eyes everything connects.

6.
Love equals gravity. A net. Handful of ocean
your mother carried in her belly, and with
your father warmed over hearth's glowing coals
to brew you. You kicked, swam, grew fins

and tail, feet, visage and soul: love's phylogeny.

Mother's fingers, woven behind your skull
fragile as an egg, held you as she sang you awake.
Each word caught. Your lovers' sure hands
will unravel the web to spin you new. It all

gives way the day you fall all the way to age.

SISTER MARY APPASSIONATA LECTURES THE PRE-MED CLASS

1. A Lesson in Anatomy

500 million years ago Mother Eve
suffered a terrible blow from God's
left hand. The top of her spinal cord,
wriggling like a snake, swelled
into a brain the size of two apples.

The vagus nerve ties head to heart,
body to soul. The brain makes us
both angel and beast, cynic and believer,
its tortuous corridors are endless, tubing
to cool the furnace of the heart.

The body's a vertebrate, its skin
and sinew dressing barest bone, but
the head's a crustacean, bony shell
encompassing memory, idea and will,
sweet meat that lies inside, making us

wise as the sea. Without memory we'd
read the same story every day, never
chilling our pleasure by seeing
the beginning with the last things
in mind, love the very same lover

over and over the first time, wake
each dawn wonderful and eloquent as Adam.
The splintered teeth and shins of saints
endear them to us. Charred timbers
of the ancient room we were born into,

bones are most enduring.

2. *Figures of Love, Spending Our Lives*

Each cell's the image and likeness
of the wriggling, snake-tailed Adam
and the apple-sweet, blood-plump egg
of Eve who came together in a garden
of their love the day it all began.

An act of love plugs in the universe
again, strews eels, oysters and salmon
under the seas, toadstools and lilies,
rams and ewes over fields, portraits
of two parents on every bedroom's wall.

Onan the Canaanite? What a waste.
The figures of love are counted always
in twos, above and below, behind
or in front, recto, verso, in and out.
Love's the one heat of every race,

lover and beloved against the clock.
The Flood rose over us because it grew
too easy for women and men to love
themselves. Cursed be they who spend
their lives in puddles on the ground.

3. *The Four Fluids*

Chemistry informs us, quickens even
the dead. Four fluids God gave Adam
combine and recombine, gurgle
and roar, simmer and cool even as we do,
in the body's labyrinthine tubes.

Blood. Dark as well water when it
pools, deep enough to drown us all.
A race's history smeared thin as dust
over the pathologist's slide, life
inscribed, unfathomable as the tides.

Milk. Blood filtered by the loveliness
of breasts, kiss of aching nipples soft as
baby's breath, one of love's recurring
wounds, smooth as the belly rounded
and taut. In a frigid world, it's fire.

Tears. Blood conducted through canals
of sense: touch, sight, scents, listen
and sing. Juice fermented from fruit
of generation. It's how we pronounce
our sentence, mourn the receding sea.

Semen. Blood boiled, concentrated in
love's retort. Man's acrid dew. God's
manna brightening our fields even as we
sleep and love, live and breathe. Yeast
we rise by. Puddles of the sea that spawned us.

4. Doctrines of the Breath

Long as we live we just can't overtake
the heart, which, even when it's resting,
strokes four times faster than the lungs.

Life culminates in exhalation. The last one
bears the soul, which flies out whistling
like a dove to search for solid ground.

He's a fool who, all ears, spends his life
listening, knowing every breath could be
the last. Only to listen means too much

gets by. Shamans breathe so fast they learn
to fly and see all things. Slow respiration
means no passion. The deepest meditation, only

time we reach the peace each of us seeks,
a place of hibernation cold as bone or snow,
only time we're really holy, means

no breath at all.

5. Bacteria and Weather, Treasure and Bones

Our dead we give back to bacteria,
beetle, grub and worm, who carry them
back to the elements, earth, water,
fire and air, where they're born again
into feather and snail, desert flower,
moss and star-dew, mildew, fog and wind.

Their softest breathing becomes all
our weather. Their burrows and barrows
are our valleys, their mounds our hills.
Rivers carry them back to us, away.
What we build they bear the weight of.
Every well and foundation we dig

reapportions the treasure of their bones.

6. The Nature of Love

Because God couldn't figure how to be
everywhere He invented mothers. Women and men

are the only animals that drink when there's no
thirst, love in and out of season, recognize
the lineaments of God beneath a lover's clothes.
God made us pupils, gave us rods and cones so we

could really see. Billions have gone, millions
today are on the way because they can't know. Love.

The paramecium, which needs no other to work
its history, still seeks out others like
itself, powerless to couple yet groping, clumping
through life's utter night toward love. Every fossil

solves for us part of love's puzzle, stones
and bones that bore us all the way from sea and tree

to now. Lovers wind like strands of protein,
dance of the double helix, Eve and Adam every time
again. It wounds and heals, drum of heart's systole
and diastole, urgent peristalsis of flesh and soul.

7. *The Nature of Vision*

Look at a woman in that certain way
and you've already known her. (It was
a son looked on as a god who first saw

this.) Too much selfishness can drive
the young or old man blind, his eyes
clenched tightly as a fist. Because

we would not see, God grew mad enough
to spit, changed our dust to mud,
rubbed it on our eyes. Leonardo

saw that the artist's vision could
light the world. Hume showed us
we could look our Maker right in the eye.

No one's as wise or eloquent as the eye.
It knows seven million colors, every
variation of night and day. We've only

so many words. Every feature of the heart's
terrain grows visible to one whose
shortsightedness has been corrected for by

love. Fleeting omens of our incipient blindness,
every sneeze chills, stills the heart, on
every pair of eyes calls down the dark.

Age? The blossoming astigmatism, last
great cataract, evening racing over fields,
sea beneath the storm, the starless night.

8. Last Things

In the graveyard late at night, ear
to the ground, you can hear the dead
squeal, grunt like boar and sow, crackle
like fat dripping from the roasting spit

of time, burst like May seed pods,
speak your name in a parent's voice.
Most men slip into earth's hard sea
whispering their mother's name, most women

their father's. In death a woman bleeds
under each horned moon, a man stays hard
as on the wedding night, both of them
sweating as if in fever or love.

In three years the coffin explodes
from all the nails and hair, every body's
progeny. Death will come at you
like no other lover, whipping your face

with her long hair as she rides you
away, man, bony thighs gripping you
hard, her voice a storm tormenting
the pine-tops, plunging his icy hand

between your limbs, woman, teeth and tongue
lightly at your throat, whispering "It's never
felt this way before." Death's got
many lovers, no friends but the crow and fly.

Some soils keep you plump and firm
forever, others suck you dry in just one day.
The higher the clouds, the better you weather;
the deeper the grave, the better you keep.

SISTER MARY APPASSIONATA LECTURES
THE NEUROLOGY CLASS

If woman and man are willful, mindful hunks
of tissue, blood and bone, what is it wills, minds

them? If they're wills and minds embodied to make them
real enough to move to love what is it embodies them?

For two years Soviet scientists with stainless blades
sliced up Lenin's brain, yet learned nothing about

learning. Technicians splattered Walt Whitman's
brain on the laboratory floor and tried to claim

it was an accident. Is knowledge the last supper?
Worms learn tricks by feasting on worms who've already

learned. So do we cannibalize our past. The flash
of light erupting in the neural cell bright as

Venus rising or stars falling from heaven rescues us
from caves of skull, root and bark of limbs, blazes

into thought, a gift of fire, we think, we know.

The Appassionata Doctrines

SISTER MARY APPASSIONATA
TO THE PALEONTOLOGY CLASS:
BEFORE THE INVENTION OF BONE

It was 510 million years ago today
that scales of calcium phosphate
blossomed on fish. Before that,
grackles and songbirds, doves and hawks
hung limp as snakes from branches,
masses of entrails that obese priests
would unreel on eves of anything proposed,
erection, election, migration, pilgrimage.
Auguries all the same: *I wouldn't*
if I were you. It doesn't look good.
Odds are against it. Not your day.
Beware, beware. There was no question
of music, no matter what the wind,
no lust to try next horizons,
grass that was greener,
only standing pat in slough and mire,
admiring finite seas from each shore.
Sooner or later all beings
went an ounce too far and collapsed,
imploding to blobs of rag and gore,
puddles of fatality. Each body
meant tent without pole, temple
of Solomon without Hiram's timber,
oak lacking bole. And in the end
death left nothing to remind,
to be polished and worked
into timeless art, next to flesh
what we hold most dear, our heritage,
this obdurate life of bone.

55

SISTER MARY APPASSIONATA
TO THE MUSIC THEORY CLASS

In ancient France

growers would crucify
a large starling

in the midst of their vines
to startle away
several acres

of its ravenous tribe
with a great death-cry.

Not every note

of every song must call on
urgent imperatives

of territory, lust
just to beget.
All songs are sad.

Like mute swans,
when we sing

if we care to be true
we must cry nothing less
than our own death,

whistle of the last breath,
screeching of each nail,
stillness of all starlings.

SISTER MARY APPASSIONATA LECTURES THE BIBLE AS LIT CLASS: *MEDITATIONS ON THE LIFE OF NOAH*

1.
Along the Ganges and Indus
it was Manu, between Eden's

Tigris and Euphrates it was
pious King Ziusudra, later

Utnapishtim, teacher of Gilgamesh,
all of whom, like our Noah,

were made to mean forever
because someone had to

invent boats and tales
once we lost our gills and fins.

2.
Legends say the ark had three decks,
lowest for animals, middle for
birds, topmost for humans, in twos

of course, but sexes kept separate
for there was penance going on,
woman's place and man's divided

by gargantuan corpses of Eve and Adam,
and still today we assign
our children rooms by myth, one parent

apart, above all beasts though we
think too well to be as good, above
even birds though we soon forget

the one song that tells us who
we are, able only in wildest dreams
to believe bone and guts can fly.

3.
Noah invented craft, the art to take
measurements exact enough to make
a near-perfect fit, courage

to take no stock in the braying
of unbelieving neighbors, patience
to wait out the worst heaven could let fall.

To him there was something wonderful
in trees, in earth's beastly stench,
a symphony in wings of flies, doves.

Heaven's spite had to dry, he knew.
He rediscovered nakedness, madness
of too much wine, invented the son's

laughing scorn. When he died he went
astonished, his tools proving useless,
age the flood there was no ark for.

SISTER MARY APPASSIONATA
TO THE WOMEN'S STUDIES CLASS:
AN ANGEL THRUSTS A SPEAR INTO
THE HEART OF SAINT TERESA OF AVILA

*After the death of St. Teresa her heart was found to bear a
long and deep mark.*
> —Butler's Lives of the Saints

*Je suis d'accord...que sainte Thérèsa est bien morte d'un
transport d'amour*
> —Dr. Jean Llermitte

Born outside the garden on the border
between too much heat and cold, conceived
as some of us are as the dream of two dreamers,
she was no stranger to angels or desire.
But this one was hard enough to make her
cry: muscle and sinew, hands rough as
any father's, knees as sharp. Not one
of Fra Lippi's urchins mugging for the artist,
wings jutting ludicrously from shoulderblades,
or Raphael's precious pudgy babies. This one
had business to carry out. He came
out of the dark, every saint's heaven and hell,
the shape and shade of holy. At first
she thought to hold him off with words.
She asked to be anyone, anywhere else.
His face flared up like a kitchen match
at midnight. In his left hand he hefted
the spear, its tip burning like shame.
Again and again he hit her heart hard,
hurting like nothing before. No
indifferent beak, heaving bull-meat, no
gold shower, but close enough. His heat
was understanding. It filled her. What
earned her such burning? A gift
for recognizing all that can be without being
seen. What remains? The tombstone row

of years leading to dust, fistful
of ash and char, a life memoryless yet
unforgotten, composed of columns of type
in so many books, stilled, scarred heart's
eternal echo, utter nothing of love.

SISTER MARY APPASSIONATA LECTURES
THE EIGHTH GRADE BOYS AND GIRLS:
A CONCISE HISTORY OF WITCHCRAFT

*For rebellion is as the sin of witchcraft, and stubbornness is as
iniquity and idolatry.*

—I Samuel

1.
The accused were stripped and bound and whipped
severely, then shaved and examined for the devil's
fingerprints. The instruments of torture
were blessed thoroughly by a priest—so often
hurt's administered and performed as a rite. Next
the victims underwent *strappado, squassation,*

thumbscrews, leg vises, Spanish boots, choking pear
and roasting chair, smoldering, sulfurous feathers
applied to underarms and groin, forced feeding
of herring soaked in brine with denial
of water, baths of slush and smoking oil, gouging
of eyes, ripping out of nails, teeth and hair,

hacking off of privates and nose, splintering
of toes, while judges interrogated them and scribes
painstakingly recorded each reply. This shows
that mankind has always been obsessed with asking
all the wrong questions, knowing all it needs
to know of religion and anatomy and tools,

writing and the law, nothing about love itself.

2.
Artificial insemination? Nothing new. For ages
succubi have drawn out semen from the man who
too much loves himself, and incubi have poured it
into the slumbering womb of the woman who wants
nobody else. Thus, like the gods themselves,

a woman and man may be virgins and at the same time
mothers and fathers, technically. And always
mothers and fathers prove themselves by the lives
of their daughters and sons to be either
angels or demons, merely human or divine.

3.
We're meant in everything we do to keep it
clean, of course, but it's *ritual* that's next to
godliness. St. Gregory tells us how a devil
entered a nun as she was eating lettuce. She'd

washed the lettuce and her hands, but forgot
to cross herself, to be reminded of the loss
of life it takes to make us live,
fathers, sons and holy ghosts, virgins, mothers,

the myths and deaths it takes to animate us.

4.
Nine knots govern potency, Virgil writes.
Witches know how to tie and untie the strands
of what we are, double helices of generation.
When a man becomes too soft to love, a woman
too high and dry, narrow and tight, when one of two

becomes too suddenly unlovely in the other's
sight, it means a witch at midnight in front of
a dying fire has tied and knotted a leather strip.
The ligature remains until the knots are found
and loosened. Fifty ways there are to tie

the knots, to diminish urination, copulation,
procreation. If you know no sorcery, just
have patience. Time too hates, and can tie knots
to weaken the force of every stream, damn
the flow, wither the heart's bouquet, make

a potter's field of every meadow, a desert of each bed.

SISTER MARY APPASSIONATA LECTURES
THE STUDIO ART CLASS:
DOCTRINES OF NAKEDNESS

1.

In Greece each cynic trotted about caked in mud,
lifting leg like bitch and pit-bull, believing only
what could be mounted, perceived, taking on in time
the hue and shade of grave. Apollo's healing rite
meant nude virgin administering balm to nude patient,
proving art can make us whole. The Israelites
lost their shirts to the gold calf, and David lost
wife and kingdom to earn the right to sing unmuffled.
One disciple ran naked into night because of Judas' kiss.
The Iroquois paired off to dance uncovered together
to bring down on field and forest the sweat of the spirit.
To lovers and mirrors going bare's the loveliest wisdom.

2.

Even Luther undressed to scare off
temptation. There are times
when this earth's so cold
even a lightning god must be
wrapped in swaddling clothes
until death casts lots for
his seamless garment. Thus
still today in graveyards
we drape our angels in folds
of stony white even though,
like Adam, Eve and us, they
haven't a thing to hide.

3.

The Middle Ages knew four ways of human revelation.
Nuditas naturalis meant Eve and Adam before they went
down, babes, morons and savages who couldn't comprehend
the lies in which women and men try to cloak themselves.
Nuditas temporalis, nakedness of each of us before
chance and law, rattling bones of poverty, fate,

snake-eyes of age. *Nuditas virtualis* signified
the clarity of the seer, unadorned truths of the good,
anchorites, dendrites, pillar-sitters embracing God.
Nuditas criminalis was the sin of sins, hot lovers
bearing passion before all else, flaming sword
and molten sheath, hell of knowing our mortality too well.

FROM EXILE, SISTER MARY APPASSIONATA WRITES TO THE CREATIVE WRITING CLASS

Any one of these three things
will make you close to God:

a sickness so hot and loud
your mouth can't spit or pray,

can't make excuses, forgets
the usual things to say; a flight

across a distant border to a land
where music's spoken and wonder's

the rule, where you need to look up
everything before you say a word;

a place to rest six feet deep, just
your size, dug with hands you've

made holy by teaching them work,
all your life to help you find the way

to care for and say, gesture and sign
of kindness, craft, every right word.

SISTER MARY APPASSIONATA LECTURES
THE CREATIVE WRITING WORKSHOP:
THIS DANCE

This witless spasm, wince or shiver,
an act natural as birth, gasp, rigor,

dangerous as the nocturnal migration
of songbirds, lark's trill circling stars;

this coma, the computer stuck fast
in an endless GOTO loop, no way to save

our labor but to crash; reckless flight
of the passion-addict too deep into lands

of ego ever to get back, heart and mind
held in every other's deadly grasp tight

as the Gila monster's jaws, shaman-trance
of pure madness: in fits and starts,

loop and whorl through every page's
wilderness, this dancing of the hand.

SISTER MARY APPASSIONATA LECTURES
THE HEALTH CLASS:
TO KEEP THE BLOOD FROM RUNNING COLD

You'll need a lover with warm hands,
with other things to do but the desire
to stay, with the belief there's nowhere
holier than the space your body takes.
Enough salt and spice for the most jaded palate.
A little too much wine. Some great fear
rumbling like empty boxcars up and down
your spine, echoing from skull-walls
like trashcan lids, screaming through
rooms of your heart like cats driven mad
by night and love. One or more young ones
in your image and likeness whose eyes
grow brighter the murkier yours turn,
who rise blazing each dawn as in
each morning mirror you shrivel and burn.
An enemy who goes to bed yearning,
unloved and alone, who prays to God
to chafe and chill you with the winds
he's known. A God who doesn't listen.

SISTER MARY APPASSIONATA LECTURES
THE FORESTRY CLASS:
DOCTRINES OF THE FIR

Hewn and hollowed out, it galloped
through faults in Troy's complacent walls.
Hallowed, it upheld in Solomon's temple
the weight of a mountain god's blustering.

Also heaven's revenge: a fir tree
split by lightning reminds us
of death's flashing hatchet.
of the days our parents were cut down.

Only try to survive, it signifies.
Seeds of a cone grown straight up
ensure success in any endeavor,
gamble, toil, gambol, pleasure.

Sister to the death-yew, it's filled
with light to celebrate, each year's close,
love's bright heights and birth's shining,
the innocence of all things young.

SISTER MARY APPASSIONATA EXPLAINS TO THE CLASSICS CLASS WHY SO MANY OF THE GREAT LOVERS, HEROES AND SAINTS WERE SHEPHERDS

Standing watch against the very dark, flock
stinking, bleating below while above it all
the head bursts with light, vast dance of planets,

harmonies of stars. Out of nowhere thrash and snarl
of assassin and prey, blood's ineradicable cry
gushing from matted wool, gathering in pools deep

as fear. Winters too cold for feeling, breath
becoming art before one's eyes, life a fire
of imagining, perfect lovers, God's reedy tenor.

August nights where the greatest torment means
to be clothed, rain hissing names of the body's
godlike parts, nothing to pattern breath upon but wind,

nothing to believe but seasons, night and dawn.

SISTER MARY APPASSIONATA RESPONDS
TO QUESTIONS FROM THE FLOOR

Q.
Can God make a stone so heavy
He can't lift it?
A.
Yes and no.

Q.
If God knows the future
how can anyone have free will?
A.
I'm not at liberty to say.

Q.
What's an eternity?
A.
We haven't the time
to go into that.

Q.
Why did God make us?
A.
Looking and hearing,
tasting and smelling, touching
to wonder. To do what we're
born for, love, to question.

SISTER MARY APPASSIONATA LECTURES THE SOCIAL BEHAVIOR CLASS: *FRIENDS, THOSE WHO LOVE*

Friends assemble to converse,
recall, chant litanies of doing,
having done, perhaps someday.
Friends must share, are just to compare,

while those who love must too soon
come to ache, measure life in strokes
on strop, whir of grindstone, consuming
by frictions, breath-song, tongue,

morning the final glassy stare,
and know in every separation the demon
of ice and bone who means them
darkness, sleeps beside them

all the way to dawn, shadows them
on either side of noon, whispering
*There's nothing beyond flesh and blood
but nothing.* Living only as they dream,

lovers are to mourn.

SISTER MARY APPASSIONATA LECTURES
THE NATURAL HISTORY CLASS:
LOVE AND CURSE, THE WIND, THE WORDS

Jesus rained on the dust his Father
made us of to brew a healing love

to teach us how to see, spat on ledgers
of the businessmen trading in the temple.

It's the sign to change our luck
or extinguish the glitter of the evil eye.

We wet the hook to lure the catch,
the hands to fit them to our work

or save them from the flames, fingertips
to learn the truth about all wealth.

It's the way to soothe any wound, sting
or burn of love too artless or old,

to show us where the wind's been before
it comes to drop us in our tracks, a blessing

to move us on, rain that sings us underground,
that makes the words of life again.

SISTER MARY APPASSIONATA
TO THE BIBLE IN TRANSLATION CLASS:
RITES OF PURIFICATION

To turn every light back on
in the house where someone
of your own tribe by his own hand
grew heavy enough with despair
to fall through his shadow, to cleanse

the hands you used in loving one
who felt loving you was but an act
or rite, brew over a fire on which
a shadow's never fallen the water
of purification squeezed from

the fat of a heifer without spot
who's known no yoke, blood of
parturition, spit and sweat
of an honest day's work, tears of love
old and brackish as the primal sea.

Stand in sun to make your shadow
do all that you do. Bathe the parts
lost to selfishness, scour the stain
of hurting others. You and shadow,
dance the sin away; drink what's left.

Remember: like cures like. Hurt
and curse can be purged only
by the flood of remembering, rite of
keeping alive the spirit of every dead,
the holy wind of every kind word.

SISTER MARY APPASSIONATA SPEAKS DURING THE RETREAT OF THE EIGHTH GRADE BOYS AND GIRLS

Three entrances to the world of fire:
slip of zipper; blouse gaping too wide
or at the wrong time; the mouth, lips,
tongue wagging with the latest passion.

You don't believe in flesh's urgencies?
Hold your hand two inches above the candle's
tear-shaped flame, or place your lips
on a sighing lover's flushed throat, then
tell me beauty doesn't move you, art,

blood, bone and skin don't matter.
Lot's daughters were forced to take the law
into their own hands. Potiphar's wife
spent her nights wrestling a eunuch.

For what she did who are we to blame her?
Dominic Savio and Teresa tried to stay saints
by forcing their eyes away from loveliness,
crying to put out every fire. They only
gave themselves headaches. Even the Savior

had an eye for beauty. The young lovers
found the morning after twined in sin,
rigid and blue with nature's last rapture,
eyes glassy with passion, the exhaust

of the '57 Chevy clogged with snow
in the drift they'd backed into in their haste
to age, clothes thrown around the back seat
like crumpled Christmas wrapping? They
lost their minds, perhaps, and we their names,

but the goodness they gave to one another,
dexterities of love, the fire they made
by moving limbs together, long as together
we live and breathe, never will grow cold.

SISTER MARY APPASSIONATA
ADDRESSES THE V.F.W.

...and the land cannot be cleansed of blood that is shed
therein, but by the blood of him that shed it.

—Numbers

The madness of the blood! Only blood
erases its own signature, only more,

drop subsumed by handful, as forest crowds
inundate each man-shaped ash or pine,

the ounce irreclaimable in the pool,
until through streets of Saigon, Teheran,

Belfast and Beirut a torrent bears away
your door, every neighbor, stains

children of rich and poor, lover's
bed and nursery floor, gushes from between

thighs of swollen wailing wives, wounds
blooming on flesh of gods and men

made breathless by hate's perfect stench,
the tongue severed, an artless stub,

until in time like fragile arteries around
every naked liver, spleen and heart

every river running to the sea runs red.

SISTER MARY APPASSIONATA LECTURES THE ARCHITECTURE CLASS: *DOCTRINES OF THE WALL*

For the stone shall cry out of the wall and the beam out of the timber shall answer it.

—Habakkuk

In the city where sons come back
to mother's house legless, armless, prone
only because fathers did before them
all walls are wailing walls.

Walls raised to separate east
of sister from west of brother, beds
of dreamers, lovers, virgins, must
be toppled. Walls are strongest things

we know, stout enough to bear the wind,
windows full of heaven, nights
of hunters, bear and swan, gourds
of moon, masterpieces of each dawn.

Refuge, siege, prison, sanctuary,
sight and blindness, law, law, law—
walls inscribe all human needs.
It only matters where we're made

to stand, how soon we need to leave.

SISTER MARY APPASSIONATA ADDRESSES THE PSYCHIC RESEARCH GUILD OF MARION, OHIO

So much that could save us, solve us
the high muckamucks won't let us near.
At Wright-Patterson A.F.B. in Dayton
in a maximum security hanger
guarded by vicious pinschers and pit-bulls
and DNA-seeking death rays
the Air Force has suspended
in liquid nitrogen three Venusians
whose saucer, disabled by acid rain
and fluctuations in the ozone levels
came down hard on Route 71
midway between Akron and Cleveland.
The Governor of the State of Ohio
and the Adjutant General
of the Ohio National Guard know this
yet consistently ignore my letters
and fail to return my calls.
What are they afraid of?

Two out of every one hundred babies
born in the U.S. come into the world
wearing a tail; one in every ten thousand
arrives gilled, finned and scaled,
trailing oozy weeds from the primal sea
like clouds of glory; recently
near Toledo a child was born
with wings, a white robe and halo.
All this is irrefutable evidence
for and against evolution.

Only art won't lie. We can read
even after desert eons in statues and paintings
what ailed Amenhotep IV:
hyperpituitarism and t.b.,
hypergonadism, acromegaly (or perhaps

chromophobe adenoma) and,
it should be pointed out,
many many centuries of utter peace.

Women give off numerous
spiritual secretions which regulate
life and love, Eastern texts
assure us. In all, fifteen
have been named, but there's a sixteenth
which has been kept secret.
Why this conspiracy of silence?
What are men afraid of?

Let them fluoridate our water,
jam our brain waves
with their state-of-the art transmissions,
abuse our weather with fly-bys
of Io and Uranus.
We're saved, each night journeying
out of the body to go where we will,
each dawn born again into flesh
by the most human instinct,

this frantic lust just to believe.

SISTER MARY APPASSIONATA LECTURES
THE URBAN STUDIES CLASS:
GUNFIRE, BEDROOM, PASSION'S TRASH

Can gunfire rattle like bone dice
in carryouts, motel rooms and bars;
sirens rise like startled city pigeons,
fumes from tired foundries over shattered faces
of the poor reflected on midnight rivers,
churn of burning urban currents, when we love?

Why, we ask, so much piggishness and rage
in bedrooms and kitchens, blood on the hands
of businessman, bureaucrat, citizen and priest?
Hate still hides itself in long white sheets,
earth ripped open to hide our every sin,
corpse after corpse borne to dust,

passion's trash.

SISTER MARY APPASSIONATA LECTURES
THE JOURNALISM AND METAPHYSICS CLASSES:
WHO WHAT WHERE WHEN WHY?

Moving down the crowded aisle, rush hour,
the No. 22 bus careening along Lorain Avenue,
pot-holed and congested, toward Cleveland's
downtown and an honest day's work, you think
you move due east, but everything you pass

hastens west, while the ancient planet
you inch across spins like a carny wheel
at the Cuyahoga County Fair, shifts like
the Tilt-a-Whirl with well-greased weight
of each and every season, running circles

around Old Sol, who too must spin, spin,
hustling through creation's eerie ether
while its Milky Way through other galaxies
pours like dregs of the pail's soapy water
emptied down the steepest gravel drive,

and for all you know this universe dances
like an Italian father drunk at his daughter's
wedding through a trillion others. In
the midst of such ceaseless velocities,
where's balance? Who can navigate for long

this labyrinth of parallax? When you've
used up all your day's light, soul and body
hurtling into night like a commuter train
twenty minutes late through a sudden tunnel
or a corpse swan-diving into earth's sea:

Just *who* do you think you are?
What will you come home to after all?
Where will you find yourself by dawn?
When did it hit you you were lost?
Now tell my *why*.

SISTER MARY APPASSIONATA LECTURES THE BIOLOGY CLASS: *NATURAL SELECTION AND THE EVOLUTION OF FEAR*

After each day's light lumbers off
to wallow into extinction and we climb
into foliage of our mammal sleep,
the winds of three dreams rise to chill us,
scents of the only three fears:
Darkness, Falling and Snake.
We recall the hankering for blood,
hearts howling at the fat moon,
stars beyond our limbs clustering
into myth. Fresh flesh quickens
the pulse, loosens tongue,
but words still choked back
to grunts, drowning in bitter froth.
One by one we reach in dream an inch
too far, night winds whistling a lullaby
in our ears, last song caught
in the throat. One terrible reptile
waits at the foot of each tree,
jaws opening on a greater dark.
Here's the enemy, since that dawn
we crawled ashore. Yet our fathers
offer a light bright enough
to burn such phantoms
from the most restless sleep.
They teach us to believe
living means never letting go
no matter how sweet the wood and fruit
of home, how great the urge to fly,
and falling, they say, must last forever.

SISTER MARY APPASSIONATA LECTURES THE QUANTITATIVE ANALYSIS CLASS: *PROOF OF THE EXISTENCE OF THE SOUL*

For nine months weigh
everything you take in:
knowledge and refreshment,
medicine, love and wind.

Over the same period weigh
everything you lose: savor
of every word, signature
of each breath, mists of life.
The difference means your very soul.

SISTER MARY APPASSIONATA QUIZZES
THE PHYSICS CLASS

What warns the circle
to stay away from corners?
Draws dusk from each dawn?

Reminds every hawk
the end of falling must
ever be to rise?

Tells scent and spore
love insists they give
themselves to every wind?

Warns each shadow
never to move between
a something and its light?

SISTER MARY APPASSIONATA
TO THE HOME EC CLASS

There is a popular conception that most nations have the cuisine they deserve.

—Food in History

1.
Horace swore that a fat hen
drowned in finest wine tasted

something like love. Death's
the spice. Eating merely to live

renders us nothing but old bones,
blood pudding, meat tough

as year-old jerky. We must
rattle those pots and pans

to make a joyful thunder, frighten
off demons of deadly habitude.

Cooking's our art most spiritual
and earthy, unvarying good taste

made of fire and time. Hunger
means some dying, each bite and swallow

like each breath, a reprieve.
Along the 9th century Rhine

ergotism taught the ravenous folk
how bitter could be their portions,

deadliness of this our daily bread,
in each crust 20 poisons, even LSD,

their bodies hot as ovens, a rash
of mad visions of the eternal place

we're remanded to, without hunger,
by the sentence most mortal:

For this is my body.

2.
Plant herbs and fruit trees
in the churchyard, one trunk
and patch of leafy fragrance

between each pair of graves
so the dead will serve to satisfy
your every hunger and the end

of rooting into clay and mire
of Mother Earth will be to rise,
root, bole, leaf to sweetest fruit,

one certain cure for each disease.

3.
Like a night of love
each meal must put to the test
all five senses. Life's
savor, what we thrust or suck
between the lips, touch to tongue
must be the kind of passion
worth dying for.
The Roman gourmand,
porcine Apicius—
when he realized he'd only
10 million sesterces left,
little less than one ton
of gold bullion, not near enough
to maintain his daily ache
for wild sow, belly bulging
with live thrushes,
and brain of peacock,
flamingo tongue, roe

of lamprey, livers of pike
caught precisely midway
between the Tiber Island
and the cloaca maxima—
reclined before a vial
of poison. It was,
he swore, just before
frothing, writhing
he lay down to sleep off
this Last Supper,
the most satisfying feast
he'd ever partaken of,
bitter and sweet as life itself.

SISTER MARY APPASSIONATA
TO THE CONTINUING EDUCATION CLASS:
*THE SINGLES MESSIAH APPEARS
IN COLUMBUS, OHIO*

There's a fever on the wind,
in the blood. Don jumpsuits,
women, open to the navel
over clinging tube tops.
Let there be a riot of designer labels,
blush-on, bags and heels
too chic for words,
tan lines, coke lines,
Charlie and Tabu. Style
your hair, men, semi-Afro
or New Wave chop. Let chest hair
flourish, art rescuing nature
where necessary, balled-up sock
in Jockey briefs even,
shark's tooth necklace,
chains, chains, chains.
Know that nothing matters
but the music, Marvin Gaye to BeeGees.
You were made to do this dance,
strut your stuff
around life's teeming bar,
its intimate booths.
Mimic all things young and real.
Make eye contact. Hit
all the right lines. Small talk
only, please. Chablis. Perrier. Coors.
Whoever your partner, make sure
you get off first.
Don't even stay for breakfast.
The light of day's but the time
you're given to make ready
for an endless night.
When Judgment comes,
and it's coming soon, heaven
will be open all night long
only for the lost and lonely.

SISTER MARY APPASSIONATA ADDRESSES THE EIGHTH GRADE BOYS AND GIRLS DURING A FIELD TRIP TO THE MUSEUM OF NATURAL HISTORY AND ART

The brittleness of what the world calls art!
Only bones, ochre and gold moans, frazzled weavings

dry as corn rows rustling in flaw-blown snow.
Rooms, rooms, rooms of stone. Nothing present

outlives its seer. All things fill and bleed,
rise to stumble, ignite to give their heat away.

What are we looking for we couldn't find studying
the backs of our hands as we write, labor or pray,

lines of care engraved around mother's eyes, portraits
hung in morning mirrors, plain song of every last breath?

SISTER MARY APPASSIONATA LECTURES
THE EIGHTH GRADE BOYS AND GIRLS:
FLESH WILLING, SPIRIT WEAK

In some ways yes we're nothing but
our acts and deeds. Yet even more
we're all we haven't, what we've
done unwell, consequence of inaction:

the times we couldn't keep tongue
from singing another soul hurt,
gardens running to seed behind
too many ramshackle houses,

entire Library of Congress classifications
unborrowed or unreturned. Elections
where we abstained, resolutions
unadopted, suffering we backed

away from, grindstones it hurt
too much to keep the nose to,
days unseized, lovers spurned, times
flesh was willing but the spirit weak.

SISTER MARY APPASSIONATA
ON THE HISTORY OF HEAT

...and at once a gentle fire has caught throughout my flesh.
—Sappho

The old ones felt it as part
of every matter, *caloric*, to be
freed by alchemy or other fire,

but we've grown cold enough to see
the dance of meson on vector boson,
gaseous fire riling metal of the pot

to madden water just enough
to draw from reticent leaves tea's
utter wisdom, so real it hurts

lips and tongue to love, to speak,
so full of light our words are made
steam. Metal's the best conductor,

with electrons enough to spare.
The worst friend of heat? Nothing.
Ask any martyr, hater, lover, corpse:

flesh and bone conduct all too well.

SISTER MARY APPASSIONATA LECTURES
THE PHOTOGRAPHY CLUB:
NOTHING WE CAN'T SEE

In the beginning, sure as
too much light, darkness blinds,
but wait just long enough and night
brightens to a world we can see
well enough to dream ourselves
unold again, lovely as our parents
in their feverish wedding reel,
everyone we're kin to, their faces
looking down loving from the wall
whole again and uncorrupt, ticks
of light and color whirling
into angels who orbit the bed,
everyone who loved us loving still,
elders, ash and pine whispering
secrets to stars just beyond
bedroom walls. When we're patient
with the dark it all takes shape
and we become a part of heaven,
our heavy selves an unjust law
no longer. We learn to fly.
In time there's nothing we can't see.

SISTER MARY APPASSIONATA
TO THE HUMAN AWARENESS CLASS:
ONE FATE WORSE

Loutish soldiers joke in line
outside the bamboo hut, khaki pants
draped over their arms, scream
after scream bursting from inside.
A mother; her two daughters,
twelve and nine. Knees
wrenched apart, clothing shredded
like newsprint. Or in the cities,
Saturday-night specials and shivs,
blasted glass glistening in arc-light,
lust blunt and beastly, big
as a fist. An old one
limp as Raggedy Ann lying
beside her bed on Social Security day,
seventy five or eighty,
dollar bills and change, a few rings
worn smooth as baby skin strewn
over the floor, the invader's
footsteps clattering down stairs.
One fate's worse than death, in truth,
children, one red stain
on this scarlet earth
no god in his right mind could forgive.

SISTER MARY APPASSIONATA LECTURES
THE ETHICS CLASS

Swear no oath to mean forever.
No one's made to stay so long,
and promise unfulfilled can leave
your children full of scorn
or bloated and pale in dust,
wounds blooming red as poppies.
Don't whisper to the deaf,
race any lame. Put no obstacles
in the way of the blind.
Leave gleanings in corners
of your fields to ensure
the poor be always with you.
The want of one widow or orphan
becomes your family hunger.
It's confusion to lie
with any beast or neighbor's mate
or with yourself while others
writhe in sleep alone.
What are hands for but to worship
or work, erect the house of love?
Care too much for nothing that can be
melted down. Take care
those appointed to feast on the goat
your sins have fattened are hungry
as the tribe was wrong.
In a world of strident wanting
leftovers can kill.
Know that all things count.
What you do, each gesture
of the hand, step, melody or word
can be only right or wrong.

SISTER MARY APPASSIONATA LECTURES
THE HISTORY CLASS: *DOCTRINES OF MEMORY*

Not one of us recollects
the first nine months, two years,
when we were lamprey, toad,

lemur, ape. Ontogeny recapitulates
phylogeny—or is it the other way
around? Twenty-five million years ago

we all wore tails, and still today
we're born wagging the coccyx.
The blood never forgets. The bone.

Memory depends. It flavors
the being. Greatest wait. Just born,
what in the world can we recall

but sudden ache about the heart,
clasp, thrash of passion, dark sea
breathing all around, time's

tight squeeze, its gush, abrupt fall
to a nether world, earth too bloody,
bright for words? It's then

we mark the gathering hurt, life-
long crescendo, fugue of age.
It never fails, sure as we're born,

life adds up until we're put
in a hole the sum of life's parts.
Count with me now: every moment

you were human, every one divine.

SISTER MARY APPASSIONATA
ON THE NATURE OF SOUND

Sound is the least controllable of all sense modalities.
—Julian Jaynes

It's the sense that counts us human
more than any other. Though not
to touch can be our choosing,
veiling eyes, holding nose,
stiffened lips together tight
as the clam's in matters of taste,
try as we might ears can't be closed.

Who speaks our way, whether
to declaim *I hate you, love*
or merely *Good day to you*
we've no choice but to let
into the mind, cede an instant
of our lives to seek to understand,
become a part of all we'll know.

Even could we declare ourselves gods
as did those crewcut Mach 1 boys
who first outflew all sound, most fear,
body's rumbling percussion even,
still there are voices heard within
that rasp and coo out terror, love,
fathers, mothers speaking their minds.

SISTER MARY APPASSIONATA LECTURES
THE BIOLOGY CLASS: *HISTORIA NATURALIS*

The Master Designer's got a sense of justice; also
humor. Bluejays, raucous bullies of the treetops
mean and brutal enough to peck to death fallen nestlings
of weaker kin to gorge themselves on the innocence
of tiny eyes, over and over again are drawn to visions,
brilliant, gaudy monarch, yet can't stomach beauty

so pure, burning, retching pain forgotten the moment
such fluttering allure comes near again. There's
a lesson here, my children, to be read in the ranks
of leafy worlds above our own, whichever way the wind
blows. Starlings going north or south fashion
in their formations every letter of scripture,

chronicle of life's wish and striving, lust for light
that's purer still beyond the next horizon balanced
by the ache for home, the known. If you're too much
bothered by the persistence of flies, it's a sign
they're helping you bear in mind each instant
of their fragile lives what you're trying to forget:

sweet and meaty sense of the beast in you. Kill
one fly and two more arrive to sing its funeral.
Your own. God placed all wisdom and faith outdoors.
Walk into dawn's fields and woods with eyes and ears
open and there's nothing you won't know, nothing
you can't bring yourself to ache for and believe.

SISTER MARY APPASSIONATA LECTURES THE MORTUARY SCIENCE CLASS: *FEEDING THE DEAD*

Northern scapegoats hurled
into murky eternities of the bog
never were sent away hungry.
Mayan mortals were interred
with mouths stuffed with maize.

In graves of antique Greeks,
feeding tubes whereby survivors
once poured steaming broth
down between lips, over tongues
of their decomposing loves and dreads.

In Lagash a dead man entombed
with 7 jars of beer, 47 loaves.
The dead wax bigger than life
to walk beside us, take hands
of our children through night mists.

No matter the season. They lie
with us time and again, each dream,
battening, thriving on the feasts
we living offer, the bitter and sweet,
all our art, this damned remembering.